TABLE OF CONTENTS

I0428803

COMPETITION: A MEANS TO TRANSFORM THE DEFENSE INDUSTRIAL BASE

> Under any form of economic or political system, those at the top tend to become complacent if not arrogant. Convincing them of anything is not easy, especially when it is some new way of doing things that is very different from what they are used to. The big advantage of a free market is that you don't have to convince anybody of anything. You simply compete with them in the marketplace and let that be the test of what works best.
>
> — Thomas Sowell, Basic Economics
> A Citizen's Guide to the Economy, 2000.

The United States national security and military strategies articulate the need to transform our forces and major defense institutions to meet the challenges of the 21st century. The defense acquisition process and its industrial base comprise a significant economic institution in need of transformation to ensure that research, development, and acquisition (RD&A) efforts remain relevant to current, future, and emerging national security requirements. Transformation must include efforts to improve the defense acquisition process that would subsequently enable it to deliver products and services that provide desired capabilities. Achieving our transformation objectives requires active measures by the Department of Defense (DoD) and our industry partners to improve weapon systems research, development and acquisition. Perpetual suggestions of acquisition reform often focus on regulatory and statutory leverage and process reform. Acquisition reform, stable appropriations, and spiral development are common and valuable recommendations. Some recent suggestions include innovative ways for the government to collaborate with industry. While these recommendations would help improve the current acquisition system, few of them offer the significant benefits derived through market leverage, namely competition.

Competition can help reduce cycle times, lower costs, and improve innovation and weapon systems performance. It can be beneficial throughout the product lifecycle, from development through sustainment and retirement. Moreover, competition will become imperative, particularly early in the research and development (R&D) phases, given the growing enthusiasm for evolutionary acquisition and quicker development and production cycle times. This increased competition might allow us to achieve our objectives of fixing the process and concurrently developing the products and services that the warfighter requires. In the commercial sector and in many defense industry examples, competition not regulation compels industry to integrate advanced technologies into producible systems and deploy them to the marketplace—-in this case the warfighter--in the shortest time practicable.

THE DEFENSE ACQUISITION ENVIRONMENT

OUR WEARY PROCESS

Our current defense acquisition environment has received much harsh criticism. The population of skeptics continues to grow and includes senior Department of Defense (DOD) leaders. Consider the recent comments by Secretary of Defense Donald Rumsfeld:

> I worry about the technology base in this country. The degree of competition is declining in the defense industry. The longer the large defense contractors deal with the Defense Department, the more they become like the Defense Department—and I don't say that as a compliment. They get big and slow and sluggish and bureaucratic. ...That means that the government tends not to have the kind of interaction with the creativity and innovation that exists in our society.[1]

Such skepticism is understandable. The weapon systems development cycle is frequently characterized by cost overruns and schedule delays. These cost and schedule setbacks are sometime quite significant and measured in billions of dollars and years of delays. Furthermore, while some technologies are clearly superior to threat capabilities, other technologies are less state-of-the art than commercial equivalents. Although it may be convenient to point the finger at a "Cold War" industry, they are not solely to blame. The defense research, development, and acquisition process is methodical, disciplined, thorough, safe, and compliant if not obedient at times to government legislation and regulations. All of these are arguably valuable qualities of scientific research and system engineering, but are, in a word, slow. This same methodical process is cumbersome to many, submissive or at best acquiescent to various stakeholders, and predominately risk averse. While this risk aversion is not necessarily preferred, it too is understandable.

Some risk is always inherent in developing a new technology: It may not work as expected; it may be more costly than expected; planned production techniques may not be appropriate. Despite these inherent risks, the process and its players can be overly optimistic in the planning stages. That optimism can and often does influence our perceptions of the technological maturity of the effort and the costs and schedule required to develop a product. Our optimism can and often does influence us to underestimate the risks associated with the technical solutions and integration required to develop a product. When critiquing warfighting plans, General Richard E. Cavazos, one of the Army's great warfighters and now a senior army mentor, always offered, "The enemy has a vote." Similarly, in the weapons research, development, and acquisition process, "technology has a vote." When operating at the technological frontier, uncertainty—about both cost and performance—makes it difficult, if not impossible, to specify in advance precisely what is required of particular systems and how much such systems are likely to cost.[2] When technology is not as mature as we perceive it to be, our optimism turns to pessimism at slowed progress and partial results. The weapon system development is suddenly short on resources to mature the technology and long on risk. A competitive environment reduces the cost and schedule risks by stimulating technology maturation and its integration. When working with a sole source developer this stimulus is missing. Despite some past and recent weapons, platforms, and munitions successes, all of these aspects have exposed the defense acquisition process and our industrial base to extremely harsh criticism and created a lack of confidence among some of our most senior leaders.

THE INDUSTRIAL LANDSCAPE

In contrast to the burgeoning development costs, cycle times, and skepticism, the defense industry has proceeded through a decade of reduction and consolidations from its Cold War levels. Comprised of government and industry organizations, the defense industrial base develops, supplies, and maintains products and services for military use. For the USA, the defense industrial base includes prime contractors, subcontractors, and parts suppliers operating publicly and/or privately owned facilities supplying air, land and sea systems[3]

> When the Berlin Wall fell in November 1989 it set in motion events that eliminated the stability and surety of the Post-World War II bi-polar global community. Uncertainty became the order of the day, and the clamor for a "peace dividend" with the resulting shrinkage of defense spending impacted heavily on the world's defense industries. In the United States the members of the defense industrial base responded in one of four ways – they consolidated, monetized, diversified, or evaporated.[4]

Contraction of the industry proceeded concurrently with a fifty-one percent decline in DoD research, development, and procurement funding.[5] Today, after a decade of change and consolidation, the U.S. defense industrial base is comprised of five large prime contractors or system integrators: Lockheed-Martin, Boeing, Northrop-Grumman, General Dynamics, and Raytheon. Subordinate to these large primes, at least those firms not already consumed by the primes, are subcontractors and parts suppliers. Some analysts assert that the existing defense industrial base appears skeptical of transformation and seems inclined to continue their efforts of promoting technologies and weaponry for massed armies in a traditional force on force confrontation.

Despite the consolidation and changing landscape, the defense industry's objective remains perpetual—to generate profits, which increase shareholder value. Our commercial industrial partners risk capital and labor, two scarce and migrating resources, to generate returns on those investments. Generating profits rewards the risk takers; it is a fundamental and appropriate principle consistent with our free market ideology. And while R&D might help pay some of industry's bills, it is production and those related profits that generate industry's return on investment, satisfy shareholders, and attract additional labor and capital. It is in the best interest of our defense industrial base to satisfy their customer, DoD, and tenaciously compete with low cost, and innovative products that get to production as soon as possible. So why are there perceptions that industry is unwilling or unable to transform? Have their acquisitions and amassed structure and overhead encumbered their agility? It is possible. Do they prefer asset accumulation and jobs programs to profit? It is not likely. Regardless of reasons or perceptions, competition may best compel the sense of urgency, agility, efficiency, and innovation that DoD desires. Although these are common free market business concepts, the defense industry is unique and our government involvement further differentiates the industry from the free market. As the sole buyer, the regulator of all market activities, the specifier of the goods to be purchased, the banker, and even the court of claims, the government is fully involved and equally responsible for the bureaucratic and slow process.[6] To paraphrase DoD's Transformation "Czar", Vice Admiral (ret.) Arthur K. Cebrowski, "There is a common, understanding that the defense acquisition process is dysfunctional. But that uncomfortable feeling is exceeded by the discomfort of having to change the process to something less familiar."[7] Fortunately, our emerging government policy embraces market leverage and competition.

AN EMERGING POLICY

As the monopsony, or single buyer of defense products, the Department of Defense must establish appropriate policy to influence its unique industrial base and improve our process. At the broadest level, there are three public policy options for the defense industry: nationalization, regulation, or competition.[8] Our RDA system continues to exhibit characteristics of each option. Congress and the executive branch have made periodic attempts to create a competitive supplier base, even though perfect competition is not possible in the defense market. The architects of the post-World War II acquisition system insisted that contracts be awarded to a large pool of suppliers, moving away from the practice of "sole sourcing" that had become standard practice before the war. In 1965 Secretary of Defense Robert McNamara testified to Congress that a savings of twenty-five percent could result from the conversion of sole source procurement to competitive bidding.[9] Succeeding administrations enacted and guided the Federal Acquisition Streamlining Act over a decade ago to reform the acquisition process, streamline government regulation, and infuse more commercial practices and competitive forces.

Our current defense industrial policy intends to shape and influence the structure of the commercial sector to meet current and future national security needs via competition. Related economic objectives of the current National Security Strategy (NSS) are based on "...market economies, not command-and-control economies with the heavy hand of government..."[10] Accordingly, the office of the Deputy Under Secretary of Defense (Industrial Policy) [DUSD (IP)] has established a policy to ensure that an adequate defense industrial base exists and remains viable and competitive to meet current, future, and emergency requirements described in the NSS. DUSD (IP) supports the Administration's consistent set of standards and principles.[11] These decisions reflect a commitment to full program funding, spiral development, and price-based acquisition, where appropriate.[12] More importantly, DUSD (IP) believes that defense companies are sufficiently motivated by their commitment to defense and their shareholder base to deliver innovation and cost-effectiveness without excessive government intervention.[13] This competition policy is not just limited to the prime contractors. The Defense Department is exploring sources of less traditional defense solutions as well as international solutions to help encourage transformation in the industrial base and innovative, timely, and cost-effective products and services for the warfighter. DUSD (IP) states "singularly among all factors, competition induces innovation."[14]

THE WAYS, MEANS, AND ENDS FOR RD&A TRANSFORMATION

The objective is to transform the defense acquisition process and industrial base, one that successfully delivered a credible deterrent during the Cold War, and overwhelming combat power in the conflicts of the past two decades, into an agile and responsive industry capable of providing products in support of emerging challenges of the 21st century. In addition to regulatory and statutory influence, increased competition is a dynamic means to achieve those objectives or ends. Competitive market forces drive innovation, improve performance, accelerate development schedules, and lower costs, all of which are desirable improvements to our existing process. Finally, there are several approaches (ways) to promote competition (means) throughout the weapon system development cycle that will enable DoD to achieve the objective (ends) of an agile and responsive defense industrial base.

PROMOTING COMPETITION THROUGHOUT THE PRODUCT LIFECYCLE

COMPETITION DURING RESEACH AND DEVELOPMENT

Increased industrial competition can be beneficial throughout the defense acquisition lifecycle, provided the benefits outweigh the costs. There may be times when the savings generated are less than the costs of a second competitor, for example, a second competing production line. However, leveraging competitive market forces early in the R&D process has proven very beneficial. Furthermore, this competition early in the lifecycle may be imperative given the growing enthusiasm for evolutionary acquisition and a procurement trend that suggests more frequent but smaller production lots and less total production quantity. Early competition stimulates efforts to mature technology and solve system integration challenges. The lack of this technological maturity has certainly been a factor that has contributed to our dissatisfaction with the defense acquisition system. Consider multiple studies from the Government Accounting Office:

- DOD Faces Challenges in Implementing Best Practices, 2002.
- Better Matching of Needs and Resources Will Lead to Better Weapon Systems Outcomes, 2001.
- Employing Best Practices Can Shape Better Weapon System Decisions, 2000.
- Better Management of Technology Development Can Improve Weapon Systems Outcomes, 1999.
- Best Commercial Practices Can Improve Program Outcomes, 1999.
- Improved Program Outcomes Are Possible, 1998.

A consistent theme in these studies indicates DoD's inclination to commit to a formal program start too early.[15] Those unsuccessful program initiations were characterized by a lack of systems engineering and resulting immature technology. That lack of upfront systems engineering coupled with a lack of competition can lead to disaster.

One way to reduce the risks associated with a lack of system engineering is to conduct competitive prototyping. Competitive prototyping, or fly-before-you-buy, is a strategy that reduces technical and economic risks, while preserving the decision maker's flexibility.[16] Its goal is to solve the technical and integration challenges of a weapon system through rigorous

6

design, build, and comparative test phases before committing significant resources to production.   This approach provides more accurate costing information on the system. Moreover, as test-fix-test design improvements continue, they more accurately prepare the competitors for an orderly transition to efficient production.[17] The Joint Direct Attack Munition (JDAM) is a frequently cited example of successfully promoting competition through the development phase.

JDAM is a body strake and tail kit that enables precision guidance for standard 500 and 2000 pound aerial bombs. The program began its development in the early 1990s. McDonnell Douglas and Martin-Marietta competed as system developers integrating several emerging technologies to include the global positioning system. Competition, innovative commercial-like management, and several other factors enabled a 33 percent reduction of the estimated development cycle, a 42 percent reduction in the estimated development cost and a 50 percent reduction in the average unit production price.[18] More importantly, the government-industry team integrated advanced technologies into a producible, affordable, and extremely effective systems and deployed it to the warfighter on time. While the JDAM success offers a recent example of market forces at work, the technique of competitive prototyping is not new. In the early 1970s DoD employed this approach during the development of the U.S. Air Force's Lightweight Fighter Program (LWF).

Competitive prototyping and the fly-before-you-buy testing gained favor during the Packard era.[19] The Air Force began the development of the LWF using this approach.[20] Under the competitive prototyping philosophy, the initial funding of a new weapon system was limited, as were the corresponding limit on performance goals and military specifications.[21]

> The reason for conducting a conceptual phase of development on an unfunded basis was obviously that this method was by far the simplest, it saved time, money and effort, and sacrificed nothing of value. A cited disadvantage…was that the very small business could not compete because of the bid and study expense involved. Since that type of bidder would not qualify for the later development award, it is not clear what is gained by paying them to compete in the concept phase.[22]

The attraction of a major procurement contract would be sufficient to encourage firms to undertake the research necessary to produce the required equipment.[23] If more than one firm can produce the needed item, then the Defense Department can allow market forces to reveal the best performing, lowest cost system. As the Air Force initiated the LWF program, five manufacturers submitted proposals to the minimally funded competition—Northrop, General

Dynamics, Boeing, Lockheed, and LTV.[24] Two of the original bidders, General Dynamics and Northrop, were selected to build prototypes, which the Air Force would evaluate with no promise of a follow-on production contract. The two contractors were given creative freedom to build their own vision of a lightweight air superiority fighter, with only a limited number of specified performance goals.[25] Northrop produced the twin-engine YF-17. Their aircraft was actually internally funded and constructed in 1965 and well tested and marketed by Northrop six years prior to any formal government program or appropriation[26] General Dynamics designed the compact YF-16. The two prototypes carried out a rigorous competition comprised initially of 288 test flights totaling 345 hours.[27] Although the Northrop contender demonstrated remarkable handling qualities and was actually superior in certain areas, Air Force Secretary John McLucas announced the YF-16 as the winner.[28] It was a little faster, demonstrated better range, used a proven engine, and was considerably less expensive.[29] Although subsequent development contracts were funded for both designs, the LWF program provides a good example of the benefits of competitive prototyping. The two prototypes performed so well, in fact, that both were selected for military service as the Air Forces F-16 and the Navy's F-18.[30]

The challenge to maintaining competitive forces throughout the lifecycle increases during the advanced development phases and transition to production. Once prototypes have competed and a selection or "down select" has occurred, DoD is wedded to a single prime contractor or lead systems integrator (LSI). The opportunities to compete within that program now reside in the component and subsystems efforts. Assuming an adequate budget, the extent of this "best-in-breed" competition can depend on the prime contractor's or LSI's penchant to facilitate subcontractor competition. However, these established or preferred business relationships between the large integrators and their subcontractors may compromise competition.

Over the years many prime contractors have built preferred supplier or subcontractor relationships, often called strategic alliances. The government can benefit from these partnerships. First, the relationship might offer some cost or price advantages. Secondly, the alliance and its familiarity can foster a collaborative environment and mutual understanding between the partners of the strategic alliance and their government customer. Conversely, these strategic alliances can hinder or obstruct competition and the inherent benefits of lower cost and greater performance. While the system integrator may obtain a preferred negotiation with a subcontractor or supplier on a weapon system development, it may be at the government's expense in terms of what other competitors have to offer. Michael W. Wynne, Principal Deputy Under Secretary of Defense for Acquisition, Technology, and Logistics expresses one way of evaluating the LSI's resolve to compete components and subsystems to find the best-in-breed. "Large defense firms that perform as lead systems integrators, or as the agents of the Pentagon on major defense programs, would be rated on how they share the R&D funds among smaller firms and on how well they encourage competition among subcontracts.".[31] Regardless of the method, a solid government understanding of the market for a given component or subsystem will help best-in-breed competitions once a single lead systems integrator has emerged. A significant Army program offers further illustration.

The Defense Advanced Research Projects Agency (DARPA) and the Army are developing technologies for the Future Combat System (FCS). It is comprised of key development programs that support the Army's transformation to the Objective Force. The FCS program will develop network centric concepts for a multi-mission combat system that will be overwhelmingly lethal, strategically deployable, self-sustaining and highly survivable in combat through the use of an ensemble of manned and unmanned ground and air platforms. An FCS-equipped force will be capable of providing mobile-networked command, control, communication and computer (C4) functionalities; autonomous robotic systems; precision direct and indirect fires; airborne and ground organic sensor platforms; and adverse-weather reconnaissance, surveillance, targeting and acquisition.

In fiscal year (FY) 2001, four competing industry consortia participated in the FCS concept development. In order to field an Objective Force this decade, the DARPA-Army leadership accelerated the program and competitively selected the industry team comprised of The Boeing Company and Science Applications International Corporation (SAIC) as the Lead Systems Integrator (LSI) in the second quarter of FY 2002. The LSI will team with DARPA and the Army to prepare for a Defense Acquisition Board Milestone B decision in the third quarter of FY 2003, to begin the full system development and demonstration.

In a draft discussion entitled, "A Unit of Action White Paper, First Principles for System Development and Demonstration" the Army "provides some overarching principles under which the planning for System Development and Demonstration of the FCS should occur.'[32] There are some key tenets that address competition. First, the LSI is not synonymous with a prime contractor:

> While it is true that from a purely contractual perspective, the LSI is a prime contractor (in a prime-sub relationship with its suppliers), he cannot be allowed to act as a prime whose motivation is total vertical integration either through future mergers and acquisitions or as a result of adopting a one-way information flow. One of the recurring complaints in Concept Technology Development is that Boeing acted more like a prime than an LSI, more like an information demander

than an information supplier. Consequently, all of its actions were treated and continue to be treated with suspicion by those who would like to supply their very best to The Army, but fear that doing so through Boeing will result in loss of critical competitive advantage. These are significant concerns and must be addressed via appropriate protection of intellectual property.[33]

Secondly, the LSI uses an approved "Make-or-Buy" process, submits "LSI Make" recommendations for Boeing and/or SAIC and notifies the government prior to "Buy" Award Announcement. In essence, the LSI acts as an "honest broker."

> It is not about LSI workshare or product recognition. In fact, to truly be an effective LSI requires that the Boeing/SAIC management team, with whom DARPA and The Army have a contractual relationship of record, [to] divorce itself from its parent company in the most dramatic way possible, as soon as possible. The LSI will not integrate vertically...it will integrate horizontally.[34]

The white paper reaffirms "No Value to Vertical Integration" to further emphasize the best-in-breed competitions:

> Few things will disrupt this enterprise quicker than a violation—real or perceived—of these tenets. One of the more significant requirements, and essential to keeping the best solutions possible coming to The Army, is to treat vertical integration with utmost suspicion unless and until it is proven to be the best solution to the requirement.[35]

The Army makes it abundantly clear that the LSI's value is "not as a builder of kit, but as an integrator across the entire Unit of Action...[and] as a manager and synchronizer supplementing The Army."[36]

COMPETITIVE PRODUCTION

While the benefits of competition through the prototype phase, first spiral or evolution, are measurable, the utility of dual sourcing in production under evolutionary acquisition is less quantifiable. There are numerous studies on dual sourcing in production that have produced both positive[37] and negative[38] conclusions on the value of competitive production.[39] Multiple variables determine the costs and benefits of competitive production. These variables can include: facilitization costs, production quantities, learning curves, economies of scale, and time value of money. Most if not all of these studies occurred prior to the enthusiasm to conduct spiral development and evolutionary acquisition. Despite that lack of empirical evidence, one can intuitively test the sensitivities of some of the variables, namely scale and cost, and hypothesize on plausible outcomes of competition in the production phase.

Evolutionary acquisition may weaken the economies of scale and cost assumptions on which the benefits of production competition are based. First, the government incurs a significant plant and equipment cost for establishing the second production line. Secondly, by splitting a finite production quantity between two firms, the government reduces the ability to generate cost savings via economies of scale. The reduced economies and increased production costs can outweigh the benefits of competitive production. Three likely variables of the new acquisition frontier—lack of performance specifications, limited production quantities, and reduced production homogeneity—intuitively suggest increases in costs and decreases in the benefits of competitive production.

One of the factors inherent in studies of dual source production concerns the government's technical data rights. In the past, the Department of Defense would contract to obtain the technical data package (TDP) or blueprints and specifications of the weapons design. These blueprints and specs would spell out all the necessary technical data, products, and processes required to build the system. Today, we have moved away from military specifications or MILSPECs (what and how to build the product) to performance specifications (what we want the product to do). One can argue that this migration towards performance specifications and away from acquiring TDPs reduces the opportunities to successfully compete the production of a weapon system. The government may no longer be able to provide a second source competitor with the blueprints, specifications, and processes.

Another assumption present in cases that indicate successful dual production sourcing concerns production quantity. Production quantities include total production and the sizes of a particular production "run" or evolution. While there is no data or direct experience with our production runs of future aircraft, vehicles, or naval systems, evolutionary development suggests smaller production quantities and less homogeneity of product. Production quantities in each evolution will necessarily shrink. However, when one examines the lifecycle of our major platforms it is evident that airframes, chassis, and hulls exceed the standards set by any private or public enterprise. We keep equipment in the inventory for decades. Therefore it seems prudent to leverage competition through the evolutionary first prototype phase and select a "winner takes all" for production. Although the selection of a sole source manufacturer effectively ends platform competition, it does allow the winner opportunities to achieve economies of scale. Subsequent evolutions of the weapon system provide opportunities for further competition at the component and subsystems levels. The Joint Strike Fighter (JSF)

11

program is executing a strategy to address these challenge and capture the benefits of both economies of scale and evolutionary performance and innovation.

The Department of Defense (DoD) selected Lockheed-Martin as the winner-take-all systems integrator for the JSF. RAND's rationale to support that winner-take-all decision was based on analysis that indicated that the cost to keep a second airframe competitor or manufacturer would be prohibitive based on the relatively limited quantity of fighters that the U.S. Air Force and international partners would buy.[40] In this most recent strategy, the fighter airframe is envisioned to remain constant throughout the lifecycle of the JSF. The evolutionary development entails improvements to mission packages such as avionics, sensors, weapons systems, communications, and engines. As previously mentioned, opportunities for competition shift from the airframe or platform "winner" or manufacturer to the companies that will compete for the mission packages in subsequent phases or evolutions. This allows the JSF program to reap the benefits of economies of scale in production and enhanced system performance via competition for the mission packages. Moreover the strategy gets product to market—aircraft to the warfighter—at reduce cycle times.

While there are many benefits to this approach, there are also cost and risks. As the weapon systems capability evolves in subsequent production lots, the military must consider retrofitting the initial weapon systems produced in earlier lots. This not only entails a labor and hardware cost of the equipment or mission enhancement package, but can also require additional training for personnel and increase the risks associated with possible readiness interruptions. With any change, there are inherent risks that the mission package will require platform modifications that might disrupt the otherwise stable production process. Once this occurs—a change in the requirement, design, or process—the benefits derived by the prototype competition and winner-take-all production selection begin to disappear. The firm fixed price arrangement for a stable platform design will likely yield to a negotiation process for the required changes. Hence, the government is back into the sole source environment that it attempted to avoid via competition.

The analysis presented thus far argues that market leverage can be an overall benefit to the government when applied throughout the RD&A process. Competing two or more firms and their prototypes can help reduce the technological and economic risks early in development. Competition can also allow sole source system integrators to identify and select the best-in-breed components and subsystems in subsequent, evolutionary development and production spirals. More importantly, this chronological application of market leverage can ensure the

12

continuous innovation required to field technologically superior capabilities to counter future threats.

ENCOURAGING COMPETITION WITH NON-TRADITIONAL DEFENSE COMPANIES

The participation of non-traditional defense companies further improves competition in the R&D phase and creates additional opportunities for reduced production costs, improved development schedules, and greater product innovation. Government reform is more likely to be effective if it makes the maximum feasible use of the same competitive pressures that apply to the private sector. Although market forces reduce certainty and increase diversity, there are strong theoretical and empirical reasons for believing that they are more efficient over the medium and long term in fostering economic and social progress.[41] The Honorable Suzanne D. Patrick, DUSD (IP) asserts that,

> Most innovations have come from [lower tier] subcontractors, and we believe that about 35% of future technology enablers will come from non-traditional suppliers," said. "We must add to the defense industrial base, even though [current suppliers] serve us well. We think we're on to something. Our aim is to capture these small non-traditional companies when their motivation is highest, given the general state of the economy and the longevity of defense programs.[42]

Her objective to encourage more commercial firm participation augments several other policymakers' attempts to reduce barriers to entry and make the defense industry more transparent and accessible.

Three independent, but related studies examined ways that DoD can attract new competition to the sector from non-defense U.S. commercial firms. RAND and the Army Science Board (ASB) explored venture capital approaches to influence innovative firms to participate in the defense business. More recently this year, DUSD (IP) completed a study that surveys the sources of less traditional defense solutions and the supplier base that will support these new technologies.[43] While their methodologies and findings varied, all three studies identified ways the governments can improve its ability to recognize and attract emerging commercial firms to enhance innovation.

In January 2000 the RAND study, Seeking Nontraditional Approaches to Collaborating and Partnering with Industry, recommended that the Army establish venture capital approaches to gain better access to innovation.[44] This approach would certainly increase the Army's exposure to innovative commercial technologies, particularly information technologies (IT). It would also provide a method for expanding the participation of non-traditional companies in

13

similar areas. However, it is not a cure-all for the challenges the Army faces in finding innovative ways to partner with industry on its transformation efforts.

A not-for-profit venture capital corporation would provide the Army another useful avenue to commercial technology. But access to and funding for innovative commercial technologies is not the critical issue. The Army has substantial funding and numerous ways to gain access to innovation. It has a science and technology (S&T) program with access to innovative technologies and products. The S&T community can access innovation through a vast federated laboratory network that includes the Army Research Lab, the National Automotive Center, Draper, Livermore, and Sandia Laboratories to name a few. Additionally, the Army has access to university research centers and their associated technology incubators, such as The Institute for Advanced Technologies and Austin Technology Incubator at the University of Texas at Austin. In addition to the federal laboratories and universities, the Department of Defense has its own internal source of innovation through DARPA's efforts.

Access to innovation is important, and so is funding. The Army has allocated substantial resources with which to fund innovative technologies for transformation. In the fiscal year 2003 budget, the Army allocated $1.9 billion (25%) of its $7.5 billion of Army Research, Development, Test and Evaluation (RDT&E) for advanced technology development and advanced component development and prototypes.[45] So, if we have significant access and ample funding to acquire innovative commercial technologies for transformation, then why do we still have or perceive a challenge?

In 2001, the Honorable Paul J. Hoeper, Assistant Secretary of the Army for Acquisition, Logistics, and Technology asked the Army Science Board to "conduct a study on Venture Capital as a means of exploring technological opportunities for modernizing the objective force given future budgetary constraints."[46] The ASB convened a Venture Capital Panel and arrived at an overall finding. "The critical issue is not the generation of funding for science and technology, but the Army's ability to identify transformational, commercial technologies and policies and procedures to transition those technologies rapidly into Army systems.[47] In their study the ASB reviewed various constraints and provided some recommendations that differ from RAND's venture capital approach. The Board's recommendations included a mix of S&T advisory teams, pilot programs, and most importantly, regulatory relief.

The ASB venture capital panel recommended that the Army augment its existing S&T organization with an advisory committee and an Army technology team. Both bodies would more closely monitor commercially relevant technologies emerging from areas such as Silicon Valley. The advisors and technology team would also network with existing venture capital firms to identify mature technologies for Army Transformation. Additionally, the ASB advised the Army to initiate a pilot program focused on integrated power sources including: batteries, fuel cells, [micro electrical mechanical systems] MEMS[48] based turbines, and power management to exercise their recommendations. Moreover, the ASB recognized that the Federal Acquisition Regulation (FAR) was too restrictive to "exploit emerging commercial technologies and procure near commercial items."[49] They acknowledged the need for a less restrictive contracting tool— Section 845 Other Transactions.

An alternative to encourage competitive commercial practices early in the weapons systems development involves a flexible contacting mechanism. While the FAR allows for reasonable interpretations, it is frequently more of a hindrance than a help during the R&D phase, which entails greater technical uncertainty and more cost and schedule risk. Title 10 U.S.C. 2371. Section 845 of Public Law 103-160, commonly called Section 845 Other Transactions or "OT," provides tremendous flexibility to negotiate terms and conditions, as is often the commercial practice. Section 845 allows for collaborative yet binding agreements for weapon system development. It facilitates rapid integration of emerging technologies through the prototype phase, unencumbered by the FAR. According to the law[50]:

- The goal of Section 845 is to (1) attract nontraditional contractors who are at the " cutting edge" of technology to conduct business with the government without changing their existing business practices, and (2) to break new ground with traditional defense contractors in doing business a new way.
- Section 845 allows DoD to experiment with immense government flexibility and innovation in structuring agreements and managing programs.
- OT's for prototype projects provide the flexibility to depart from procurement contracts imposed by statute or regulation and can help integrate the government and commercial industry. Other Transactions for Prototypes are based on commercial practices and as such, are not required to comply with the FAR, DFARS, or those laws and regulations that are limited to procurement contracts, e.g. Truth in Negotiations Act and Cost Accounting Standards.

Additionally, OT 845 Agreements can cut the bureaucracy and time typically associated with a government contract that might otherwise discourage commercial firms from participating.

Prior to selecting a lead systems integrator for the Army FCS program, DARPA used Section 845 Other Transactions to encourage competition among four industrial teams or consortia. Each of these teams contained member firms that were non-traditional defense companies. Also, OT 845 enabled the competing teams to renegotiate among themselves in order to "reshuffle" the competition and build the most competitive team for the down select to a LSI. DARPA and the Army again used an OT 845 agreement to choose a LSI to prepare the FCS program for a milestone B in 2003. While not previously teamed in the earlier phase, DARPA and the Army selected Boeing and SAIC to prepare the FCS for an official development program in 2003. This allows the government additional opportunities to encourage innovation in the less traditional defense companies. Additionally, this method provides for both price-based, and performance-based prototypes as metrics. Although competition may force the cost of weaponry down, the uncertain technological environment undermines the potential for competition. After all, how can the services choose among bids to create the unknown?[51] Priced prototypes might reduce much of the technological and integration risks that cause this buyers' uncertainty and undermine competition.   It requires the competitors to take a finite amount of resources, mature the technology, integrate the subsystems, and show up on a given date, to demonstrate their weapon system. As mentioned earlier, the flexibility of Section 845 has enabled DoD to attract and compete commercial firms and consortia that have historically declined to participate in research projects because aspects of contracts, grants, or cooperative agreements have made the use of those instruments inappropriate

Despite differing methodologies and findings, the RAND, ASB, and DUSD (IP) studies all reveal a common requirement. In order to achieve the aggressive schedule and performance metrics for the Objective Force and FCS, the Army must leverage all available, traditional and non-traditional, sources of technological innovation. An Army Venture Capital approach might provide unique access to innovative commercial technologies. This is particularly helpful in the IT fields that are vital to the FCS and network centric warfare. However, a less unique but more productive method entails augmenting the Army's S&T community with expertise to identify and assess maturing commercial technologies that have relevance to defense transformation. Furthermore, these methods would help spur the participation of non-traditional defense companies and increase the level of competition for defense programs.

The traditional defense companies currently serving the defense sector have mixed opinions about the DUSD (IP)'s aims to attract non-traditional defense companies. "There is one flaw with the plan; we don't need more companies entering the defense industrial base, because there's an overcapacity now," said L-3 Communications Corporation Chairman and CEO Frank Lanza.[52] Herley Industries President and Chief Executive Officer Myron Levy agreed. "For some reason, the Defense Department seems to believe there are no entrepreneurial companies among the [group] with whom it is currently doing business.[53] Lanza and some other small- and medium-size defense contractors complained that only a tiny share of R&D money that the Defense Department makes available to large systems integrators flows down to lower tier suppliers, choking off innovation.[54] In contrast, Northrop Grumman's Chief Executive Officer Kent Kresa supports the participation of smaller, non-traditional suppliers to counter new threats. "We in the defense industry have to become more proactive working with smaller and more non-traditional suppliers, domestic and foreign. By broadening our technology pool, we will be able to tackle the number of daunting challenges that we have."[55] Despite these risks, the focus of the policy efforts is to make maximum use of the commercial industry to enhance competition and its resulting innovation.

A recent example of innovation over institution entails Exponent, Inc. a small, innovative west coast engineering firm that replaced a big five firm and incumbent Raytheon as systems integrator for the Land Warrior in 1999. Land Warrior is the Army's integrated digital system that incorporates computerized communication, navigation, targeting, and protection systems for use by the dismounted infantry soldier on the battlefield of twenty-first century.[56] It has been under development for a decade. Exponent and the U.S. Army's Project Manager - Soldier Systems, selected the system components and the team to develop it in October 1999 and delivered the first Land Warrior system to the Government six months later for testing.[57] As the program manager and system engineer, Exponent led a six-member consortium including Cadence Design Systems, Kaiser Electronics, LEMO USA, Pacific Consultants, Point Research, and Thor Electronics through development, testing, and assembly of the pre-production Land Warrior units.[58] Using commercial off-the-shelf (COTS) technologies, Exponent and a team of innovative partner companies created the Land Warrior System Version 0.6 and version 1.0. Early in their efforts, Exponent displayed a great capability to solve some technical and economic risks.[59] Using COTS, Exponent reduced the size and weight of the electronic wearable computer and wireless LAN from 21 pounds to 13 pounds. This was accomplished in an impressively rapid design–to-prototype development cycle. They also improved the human factors engineering by separating and distributing various components from the soldiers back to the web belt and load bearing equipment straps. This rapid prototyping was achieved by using commercial practices and COTS technologies. The Army was satisfied with the rapid spiral development on a negotiated fixed price contract via an OT 845 agreement. Surprisingly, however, in January 2003, the Army awarded General Dynamics Decision Systems, a business unit of General Dynamics, a $59.9 million cost-plus-fixed-fee contract to enhance the current version of the U.S. Army's Land Warrior.[60]

What went wrong with this seemingly successful "David and Goliath" example of non-traditional defense company? Apparently, as the Land Warrior progressed through developmental testing, Exponent's version 1.0 experienced environmental hardware and software failures. The consortia reacted swiftly with their test-fix-test system engineering. However, as the test failures continued, the system engineering started to relax and the configuration management began to founder. This program is of course a sample size of one. But the Land Warrior program presents some interesting challenges to a government that shows great enthusiasm for the participation of non-traditional companies. Are small, innovative companies capable of transitioning their prototypical designs to full-scale development and testing? Are COTS components including commercial operating system software capable of the harsh environmental challenges?[61] As the lessons learned emerge from this program and a larger population of sample programs, the government will be able to establish a better track record and participation role for non-traditional defense companies.

EXTENDING COMPETITION TO INTERNATIONAL PARTICIPATION

In addition to domestic competition to include increased participation by non-defense U.S. firms, we should attempt to further increase competition by opening our defense markets to international firms. If as a nation, we seek for our military the best performing products, at the lowest possible prices, and in the quickest available times, then our efforts should include international competitors. Simple notions of comparative advantage suggest that nations will have different comparative advantages and are likely to gain from specialization and international trade: hence self-sufficiency is costly.[62] This will be particularly important should our domestic market in certain sectors consolidate to just one firm capable of providing the desired weapons system. While the government can regulate or negotiate with a single domestic supplier, there is an abundance of empirical evidence that monopoly products and services lack the price, performance, and evolutionary innovation that we desire. Furthermore, the principle of contestable markets stresses the importance of the *threat* of entry and rivalry: a contestable market need not be populated by a large number of firms (as in perfect competition) and it is contestability rather than structure that determines performance.[63] On this basis, governments can make their domestic monopoly defense industries contestable by threatening or actually opening up their national markets to competition from a few foreign firms.[64]

Along with NATO and or European Union countries, we should consider establishing multilateral agreements with secure, capable countries that have joined the war on terrorism. In most cases, only wealthy, highly stable democracies have the high technology base needed to

18

develop advanced weapon systems.[65] Additionally, by including international corporations, we further increase the area of the net we cast in search of mature, relevant technologies. Our international inclusion has some residual, yet extremely significant benefits. First, the technology gap between the U.S. and our Tier 1 allies is widening. Alliance interoperability has become an enormous challenge for all of us. We're not going to be able to keep the alliance together technologically unless we find ways for greater collaboration between our industrial sectors.[66] International cooperation and competition will help bridge the technology gap and interoperability challenges. Secondly, international participation offers a technology transfer quid-pro-quo to our trusted coalition partners who are "tracing bank accounts, sharing criminal information and other basic tasks of transnational law enforcement."[67] In other words, a global effort on technology development enhances a global war on terrorism (GWOT). We will need to leverage the GWOT to balance the increased political and economic risks associated with opening our markets to international competition, particularly in our current environment of domestic economic uncertainty.

THE CHALLENGES OF COMPETITION

While the analyzed ways of competition provide great benefits, the methods are not without additional economic and political risks. Despite reduced procurement costs in the long run, the costs to compete in development will further increase the resources required in the near term budgets. In addition, one cannot underestimate the political risks associated with domestic competition. Those challenges increase as we encourage competition through the participation of non-traditional defense and international companies.

FISCAL COSTS

Extending competition throughout the lifecycle requires planning for adequate fiscal resources to support the increased competition requirements. In a simple model, the government might require twice the resources to fund two competing sources through the delivery and demonstration of prototypes. Contracts with lead system integrators will increase and could double to enable best-in-breed competition among the component and subsystem firms. While multiplying required resources is admittedly costly, one only has to review the cost growth of major weapons systems to gain perspective. Some of those program failures or systems still under development have more than doubled their original cost estimates and resource requirements.

It is optimistic to think that DoD would request and Congress would double the procurement appropriations. A more reasonable vision is a mix of some appropriation increases and procurement cancellations or force structure reductions to provide the additional resources to fund increased competition through the development lifecycle. While it requires additional up-front resources, it will ultimately provide for a "better, faster, cheaper" set of solutions for the warfighter. On one hand, it might be possible to adequately meet US security requirements at lower budget levels by adopting a slightly smaller military, and a modernization plan focused more on transformation-oriented weapon systems. On the other hand, R&D and procurement budgets may need to increase. A budgetary increase would initially fund the inclusion of more non-defense and international companies during the R&D phase of various technology efforts. In other words, the ability of the US military to effectively meet future challenges is likely to have much more to do with how wisely we spend our defense dollars, than on how much we spend.[68] Regardless of budget totals, empirical evidence suggests that reduced regulation and the competitive forces of the free market early in development provide significant savings during the costly production phases. No matter how much money is spent on our defense, our nation will not have the agile, innovative fighting forces it needs to prevent and/or win future wars without major changes in the way the Pentagon does business.[69] In addition to fiscal resources, we must consider relaxing some DoD Directives consistent with the Secretary Rumsfeld's recent memo on reducing defense business processes.[70] Equally important, we must anticipate the need to seek additional acquisition reform through legislative changes to the FAR to assist this process. There can be no Revolution in Military Affairs (RMA) without a Revolution in Business Affairs.[71]

POLITICAL RISKS

It is too early to cite examples of congressional curiosity or inquisition, into increased competition. However, one must predict that the pursuit of traditionally non-defense firms or international firms will generate some political risk. Congressional members and the committees and sub-committees that authorize and appropriate funds for defense R&D and procurement are an inquisitive and powerful caucus.[72] Transformation could be the best thing that has happened to the military in a generation, or it could also turn into a political and budgetary fiasco.[73] One need only look at some recent examples of investigations into increased competition and the Congressional voice of the constituency that emerged. In 1997 DoD was considering a second production source for the Family of Medium Tactical Vehicles (FMTV). The FMTV is a truck produced by Stewart and Stevenson in Sealy, Texas. Certain Texas legislators took great interest in the rationale for dual sourcing. Ultimately, after much dialogue the congressional arguments for sole source economies of scale and learning curve silenced the proponents of competition, DoD, Oshkosh and AM General.[74] As the FMTV example shows, the government can demonstrate anti-competitive behavior. Indeed, public choice analysis suggests that various interest groups in the military-industrial-political complex who are likely to lose from competition will appose it.[75] While challenging the domestic defense–industrial complex is risky, introducing international participation in the same domestic "iron triangle"[76] is even more difficult. However, benefits of competition are greatest when we remove all barriers to entry, including political, social, or economic barriers to international competitors.

CONCLUSIONS

This paper presented and analyzed some measures the Department of Defense might consider to leverage market conditions and improve competition. Competition can help reduce cycle times, lower costs, and improve innovation and weapon systems performance. It can be beneficial throughout the weapon systems lifecycle, from development through sustainment. Moreover, competition will become imperative, particularly early in the R&D phases, given the growing enthusiasm for evolutionary acquisition and quicker development and production cycle times. This increased competition might allow us to achieve our objectives of fixing the weary acquisition process. Concurrently, market leverage will help DoD develop the products and services that the warfighter requires. As witnessed in both commercial and defense industries, competition not regulation, compels industry to integrate advanced technologies into producible systems and deploy them to the marketplace—-in this case the warfighter--in the shortest time practicable. The challenge for The Army in the 21st Century is to field the most modern equipment available at a time when technological advances are outpacing our ability to fully understand how these capabilities change the battlefield.[77] By easing regulations, encouraging new domestic participation, and opening our defense markets to international firms, we will create opportunities to develop cheaper, faster, and better capabilities to counter our 21st century challenges. In summary, competition is a valuable market force throughout the weapon systems development cycle. However, the process of evolutionary acquisition will require new strategies for competition. Initially, competition must be fierce to ensure high performance and low lifecycle-cost prototypes, to enable a well-informed winner-take-all decision. During the limited production phases of future weapon systems, emerging strategies will enable competition among component and subsystem producers, allowing the sole-source platform manufacturer to focus on economies of scale. Finally, the acquisition community will require great discipline to maintain a stable platform design to avoid the disadvantageous position of negotiating production changes with a sole source manufacturer. Ultimately, these strategies and conditions will enable DoD to transform the defense industrial base into one that will continue to develop, produce, and field technologically advanced weapons systems, in the shortest practicable times, and at the lowest possible costs.

WORD COUNT = 8,578

ENDNOTES

[1] " Don Rumsfeld Talks Guns and Butter", Fortune, 18 November 2002, 143.

[2] Rachel Weber, Swords Into Dow Shares, Governing the Decline of the Military Industrial Complex (Boulder: Westview Press, 2001), 48-49.

[3] Jacques S. Gansler, Affording Defense, (Cambridge: MIT Press, 1989), 239-240.

[4] Bernard F. Griffard, "Shortening The Defense Acquisition Cycle: A Transformation Imperative," Issue Paper 13-02, (Carlisle: Center for Strategic Leadership, November 2002), 2.

[5] Office of the Deputy Undersecretary of Defense for Industrial Policy, Transforming the Defense Industrial Base: A Roadmap, (Washington, D.C., Office of the Deputy Undersecretary of Defense for Industrial Policy, February 2003), 10.

[6] Jacques S. Gansler, Defense Conversion, (Cambridge: MIT Press, 1995), 24.

[7] Vice Adm. (ret) Arthur K. Cebrowski, "New Rules for a New Era," Transformation Trends, October 21, 2002.

[8] Gansler, Defense Conversion, 85.

[9] T. L. McNaugher, New Weapons, Old Politics: America's Military Procurement Muddle, (Washington, D.C.: The Brookings Institution, 1989).

[10] President George W. Bush, The National Security Strategy of the United States of America, (Washington, D.C.: The White House, 2002), 17.

[11] Deputy Undersecretary of Defense for Industrial Policy, Annual Industrial Capabilities Report to Congress, Washington, D.C., Government Printing Office, March 2002, 1.

[12] _____ Testimony Before the US HR Armed Services, Subcommittee on Procurement, , Washington, D.C., Government Printing Office, 4.

[13] _____ Annual Industrial Capabilities Report to Congress, 1.

[14] DUSD (IP), Transforming the Defense Industrial Base: A Roadmap, 35.

[15] General Accounting Office, Best Practices: Better Matching of Needs and Resources Will Lead to Better Weapon System Outcomes., (Washington, D.C., U.S. General Accounting Office, 8 March 2001), 4.

[16] Franklin C. Spinney, "Defense Time Bomb," March 6, 1996, 11, available from http://www.defense-and-society.org/fcs/pdf/defense_budget_time_bomb.pdf>; Internet; accessed 6 February 2003.

[17] Ibid., 11.

23

[18] Dominique Myers, "Acquisition Reform — Inside the Silver Bullet, A Comparative Analysis —JDAM Versus F22," <u>Acquisition Review Quarterly</u>, (Fort Belvoir: Defense Systems Management College, Fall 2002), 316.

[19] The Honorable David S. Packard was a co-founder of Hewlett-Packard and served as Deputy Secretary of Defense from 1969 to 1971.

[20] Lieven Dewitte and Stefaan Vanhastel, "F-16 Light Weight Fighter Program" available from <http://www.f-16.net/reference/versions/f16_lwf.html>; Internet; accessed 17 March 2003, 1-5.

[21] "Northrup YF-17 Cobra," available from <http://home.att.net/~jbaugher4/f17.html>; Internet; accessed 27 February 2003, 3.

[22] George A. Spangenberg," Aircraft Acquisition—Management Malpractice," available from <http://home.att.net/jbaugher4/f17.html>; Internet; accessed 27 February 2003, 2.

[23] C. R. Neu. Defense Spending and the Civilian Economy, (Santa Monica: RAND Corporation, October 1990).

[24] Dewitte and Vanhastel, 2.

[25] Ibid., 2.

[26] "Northrup YF-17 Cobra," 3.

[27] Ibid., 5.

[28] Ibid., 6.

[29] Ibid., 6.

[30] "F-16 Fighting Falcon History," available from <http://www.globalsecurity.org/military/systems/aircraft/f-16-history.htm>; Internet; accessed 26 February 2003, 2.

[31] Gopal Ratnam; "Pentagon Wants Companies to Close Excess Weapons Plants," <u>Defense News</u>, Feb 4, 2003, 1.

[32] "A Unit of Action White Paper, First Principles for System Development and Demonstration" Draft Discussion provide by a guest speaker participating it the Industrial Base elective, 1.

[33] Ibid., 16.

[34] Ibid., 6.

[35] Ibid., 17.

[36] Ibid., 13.

[37] Gansler, <u>Affording Defense</u>, 185.

[38] "Dual Sourcing in Defense Missile Procurement," Internal PA&E Draft of Missile Paper, April 8, 1987 available from <http://www.economics.osd.mil/Dual_Sourcing.pdf>; Internet;.accessed 16 January 2003, 1-27.

[39] William N. Washington, "A review of the Literature: Competitive Versus Sole-Source Procurements," Acquisition Review Quarterly, Volume 4, Number 2 (Alexandria, Defense Acquisition University, Spring 1997, 173-188.

[40] John Birkler et al., Assessing Competitive Strategies for the Joint Strike Fighter: Opportunities and Options, (Santa Monica: RAND, 2001), 1-19.

[41] Joseph V. Kennedy, "A Better Way to Regulate," Hoover Institute, Policy Review No 102 (Stanford, Standford University Press, Oct-Nov 2001) available from <http://www.policyreview.org/>; Internet; accessed October 2002.

[42] Anthony L. Velocci, Jr., "Pentagon Targeting Potential Suppliers," Aviation Week & Space Technology, 3 Februrary 2003, 32.

[43] DUSD (IP), Testimony Before the US HR Armed Services, Subcommittee on Procurement, 4.

[44] Bruce Held et al., Seeking Nontraditional Approaches to Collaborating and Partnering with Industry, (Santa Monica: RAND, 2001), 33-53.

[45] Department of the Army, "Descriptive Summaries for the Program Elements of the Research Development, Test and Evaluation, Army, FY2004/2005, President's Budget Submission," Volume I, (Washington, D.C.: Government Printing Office, February 2003), 1.

[46] Paul J. Hoeper, Assistant Secretary of the Army for Acquisition, Logistics, and Technology, "Memo Subject," memorandum for Army Science Board, Washington, D.C., January 8, 2001.

[47] Army Science Board, "Venture Capital Panel," briefing slides, July 25, 2001 available from <https://webportal.saalt.army.mil/sard-asb/ASBDownloads/Final%20VC %20Brief.pdf>; Internet; accessed 26 February 2003.

[48] Micro-Electrical-Mechanical Sensors are small devices that can provide three-axis motion information. These dual-use technology sensors are used in a variety of ways to include activation an automobile collision air bag to navigation for platforms and precision weapons.

[49] Army Science Board, "Venture Capital Panel," 19.

[50] Title 10 U.S.C. 2371. Section 845 of Public Law 103-160, FY1994 National Defense Authorization Act.

[51] Weber, 52.

[52] Velocci, 32.

[53] Ibid., 32.

[54] Ibid., 32.

[55] Edmond Lococo, "Northrop's Kresa Comments On Defense Industry Consolidation," Bloomberg.com, available from <http://ebird.dtic.mil/Feb2003/s20030205151861.html>; Internet; accessed 5 February 2003, 1.

[56] Department of the Army, 2002 U.S. Army Weapon Systems Handbook, (Washington, D.C.: U.S. Department of the Army, 2002), 119.

[57] "Exponent and Army's 'Land Warrior' System Achieves Success," Menlo Park, CA, September 21, 2000, available from <http://www.exponent.com/about/news/land_warrior 3.html>; Internet; accessed 21 March 2003.

[58] "Land Warrior," available from <http://www.exponent.com/about/news/land_warrior 3.html>; Internet; accessed 21 March 2003.

[59] Interviews with Land Warrior government program officials.

[60] "US Army Selects GD To Lead Development of Land Warrior," available from http://www.defense-aerospace.com/data/communiques/data/2003Feb14176/;Internet; accessed 21 March 2003.

[61] Land Warrior used a Microsoft Windows based operating systems that encountered numerous cursor lock-ups and other software driver and interface failures. These failures were attributed to the handling and shock conditions prevalent in a dismounted soldiers environment.

[62] Todd Sandler and Keith Hartley, The Economics of Defense, (Cambridge: Cambridge University Press, 1995), 188.

[63] William Baumol, John Panzar, and Robert Willig, "Contestable Markets and the Theory of Industrial Structure," American Economic Review, 72, (New York: Harcourt Brace and Jovanovitch, 1982), 1-15.

[64] Sandler and Hartley, 186.

[65] Ivan Eland, "Reforming a Defense Industry Rife with Socialism, Industrial Policy, and Excessive Regulation," Policy Analysis No.421, (Cato Institute, Washington D.C., 2001), 7.

[66] Jim Garamone, "DoD Concerned About Defense Industrial Base," American Foreign Information Service News Articles, November 1999, available from <http:www.defenselink.mil/ news/Nov1999/n11081999_9911084.html>; Internet; accessed 18 December 2003

[67] G. John Ikenberry, "American Grand Strategy in the Age of Terror," Survival, Vol 43, No. 4 (Oxford: Oxford University Press, Winter 2001-2002), 19-34.

[68] Steven Kosiak, "2003 Defense Budget Request: Large Increase in Funding, Few Changes to Plans," (Washington, D.C., Center for Strategic and Budgetary Assessments, 2002), available from <http://www.csbaonline.org>; Internet; accessed October 2003.

[69] Josh S. Weston, Co-Chairman, Business Executives for National Security Tail-to-Tooth Commission, Testimony to the Senate Budget Committee, February 28, 2002.

[70] Secretary of Defense Donald Rumsfeld, "Legislative Priorities for Fiscal Year 2004", memorandum for Secretaries of the Military Departments, Washington, D.C., 17 September 2002.

[71] General Dennis J. Reimer, "The Revolution in Military Logistics," Army Logistician January-February 1999, 2.

[72] The Military Procurement and Research and Development Subcommittees of the House Armed Services Committee (HASC); The Subcommittees on Emerging Threats and Capabilities , Air-Land, and Seapower of the Senate Armed Service Committee (SASC); the Defense subcommittee of the House Appropriation Committee (HAC); and finally, the Defense subcommittee of the Senate Appropriation Committee (SAC);

[73] Loren B. Thompson, "The Limits of Transformation," Washington Post, 12 March 2001.

[74] Paul Dodson, "AM General Vies for Army Pact," South Bend Tribune, 4 November 1998, 1.

[75] Sandler and Hartley, 154.

[76] The "Iron Triangle" forms the U.S. military establishment's decision-making structure and includes its major interest groups. One side of the triangle includes the "civilian" agencies that shape U.S. military policy-the Office of the President, the National Security Council, the Senate and House Armed Services Committees, and civilian intelligence agencies like the CIA and NSA. A second side includes the military institutions-the Joint Chiefs of Staff, the top brass of the Air Force, Army, Marines, and Navy, the powerful "proconsul" regional commands (known as "CINCs"), and, in a supporting role, veterans' organizations like the American Legion and the Veterans of Foreign Wars. At the base of the triangle are the 8S,000 private firms that profit from the military contracting system, and that use their sway over millions of defense workers to push for ever-higher military budgets.

[77] Department of the Army, The Army, Field Manual 1, (Washington D.C.: U.S. Department of the Army, 14 June 2001), 28.

BIBLIOGRAPHY

Abshire, David M. and Harrison, Stanley, co-chairman. "Defense Economics for the 1990s: Resources, Strategies, and Options." Washington, D.C.: The Center for Strategic and International Studies, 1989.

Anders, William A. Rationalizing America's Defense Industry: Renewing Investors Support for the Defense Industrial Base and Safeguarding National Security. Defense Week 12th Annual Conference, 1991.

Army Science Board. "Venture Capital Panel." Briefing slides, July 25, 2001. Available from <https://webportal.saalt.army.mil/sard-asb/ASBDownloads/Final%20VC %20Brief.pdf>. Internet. Accessed 26 February 2003.

Baumol, William, Panzar, John, and Willig, Robert. "Contestable Markets and the Theory of Industrial Structure." American Economic Review, 72, New York: Harcourt Brace and Jovanovitch, 1982.

Birkler, John and Smith, Giles. An Acquisition Strategy, Process, and Organization for Innovative Systems. National Defense Research Institute. Santa Monica: RAND, 2000.

Bush, President George W. The National Security Strategy of the United States of America Washington, D.C.: The White House, 2002.

Cebrowski, Arthur K., Vice Adm. (ret), "New Rules for a New Era," Transformation Trends, 21 October 2002.

Defense Science Board. 1996 Summer Study Report on Achieving an Innovative Support Structure for 21st Century Military Superiority. 1996.

Department of Defense Directive No 5000.60. Defense Industrial Capabilities Assessment. Washington, D.C.: GPO, 1996.

Department of Defense. Annual Industrial Capabilities Report to Congress. Washington, D.C.: GPO, 2002.

Department of the Army. "Descriptive Summaries for the Program Elements of the Research Development, Test and Evaluation, Army, FY2004/2005, President's Budget Submission," Volume I. Washington, D.C.: Government Printing Office, February 2003.

Deputy Under Secretary of Defense (Industrial Policy). Testimony Before the United States House Committee on Armed Services, Subcommittee on Procurement. Washington, D.C.: GPO, 2002.

Dewitte, Lieven and Vanhastel, Stefaan. "F-16 Light Weight Fighter Program." Available from http://www.f-16.net/reference/versions/f16_lwf.html. Internet. Accessed 27 February 2003.

Dodson, Paul. "AM General Vies for Army Pact." South Bend Tribune, 4 November 1998.

"Don Rumsfeld Talks Guns and Butter." Fortune, 18 November 2002.

Eland, Ivan. "Reforming a Defense Industry Rife with Socialism, Industrial Policy, and Excessive Regulation." Policy Analysis No.421. Cato Institute, Washington D.C., 20 December 2001.

"Exponent and Army's 'Land Warrior' System Achieves Success." Menlo Park, CA, September 21, 2000. Available from <http://www.exponent.com/about/news/land_warrior 3.html>. Internet. Accessed 21 March 2003.

"F-16 Fighting Falcon History." Available from http://www.globalsecurity.org/military/ systems/aircraft/f-16-history.htm. Internet. Accessed 26 February 2003.

Gansler, Jacques S. The Defense Industry. Cambridge: MIT Press, 1980.

_____. Affording Defense. Cambridge: MIT Press, 1989.

_____. Defense Conversion : Transforming the Arsenal of Democracy. Cambridge: MIT Press, 1995.

Garamone, Jim. "DoD Concerned About Defense Industrial Base." American Foreign Information Service News Articles, November 1999. Available from <http:www.defenselink.mil/ news/Nov1999/n11081999_9911084.html>. Internet. Accessed 18 December 2003.

Hoeper, Paul J. Assistant Secretary of the Army for Acquisition, Logistics, and Technology, "Memo Subject," memorandum for Army Science Board, Washington, D.C., January 8, 2001.

Ikenberry, G. John. "American Grand Strategy in the Age of Terror," Survival, Vol 43, No. 4, Oxford: Oxford University Press, 2002.

Isenbberg, David and Eland, Ivan. Policy Analysis No.442-Empty Promises: Why the Bush Administration's Half Hearted Attempts at Defense Reform Have Failed. Washington D.C.: Cato Institute, 2002.

Kennedy, Joseph V. "A Better Way to Regulate." Hoover Institute, Policy Review No 102 Stanford, Standford University Press, Oct-Nov 2001.

Kosiak, Steven. "2003 Defense Budget Request: Large Increase in Funding, Few Changes to Plans." Washington, D.C., Center for Strategic and Budgetary Assessments, 2002. Available from <http://www.csbaonline.org>. Internet. Accessed October 2003.

"Land Warrior." Available from <http://www.exponent.com/about/news/land_warrior 3.html>. Internet. Accessed 21 March 2003.

Leitzel, Jim, ed. Economics and National Security. Boulder: Westview Press, 1993.

Lococo, Edmond. "Northrop's Kresa Comments On Defense Industry Consolidation." Bloomberg.com. Available from http://ebird.dtic.mil/Feb2003/s20030205151861.html. Internet. Accessed 5 February 2003.

McNaugher, T. L. New Weapons, Old Politics: America's Military Procurement Muddle. Washington, D.C.: The Brookings Institution, 1989.

Myers, Dominique, Acquisition Reform—Inside the Silver Bullet, A comparative Analysis—JDAM Versus F-22, Acquisition Review Quarterly, Fall 2002, Ft Belvoir.

"Northrup YF-17 Cobra." Available from http://home.att.net/jbaugher4/f17.html. Internet. Accessed 27 February 2003.

Office of the Deputy Undersecretary of Defense for Industrial Policy. Transforming the Defense Industrial Base: A Roadmap. Washington, D.C.: Office of the Deputy Undersecretary of Defense for Industrial Policy, February 2003.

Olvey, Lee D., Golden, James R. and Kelly, Robert C. The Economics of National Security. Wayne: Avery Publishing Group, 1984.

Pascal, Glenn R. and Lamson, Robert D. Beyond Guns and Butter: Recapturing America's Economic Momentum After a Military Decade. Washington: Brassey's, 1991.

Ratnam, Gopal. "Pentagon Wants Companies to Close Excess Weapons Plants." Defense News. Feb 4, 2003.

Reimer, General Dennis J. "The Revolution in Military Logistics." Army Logistician January-February 1999.

Rumsfeld, Donald, Secretary of Defense. "Legislative Priorities for Fiscal Year 2004." Memorandum for Secretaries of the Military Departments. Washington, D.C., 17 September 2002.

Rumsfeld, Donald. Memorandum for Secretaries of the Military Departments, Subject: Legislative Priorities for Fiscal Year 2004, September 17, 2002.

Sandler, Todd and Hartley, Keith. The Economics of Defense. Oxford: Cambridge University Press, 1995.

Spangenberg, George A. "Aircraft Acquisition—Management Malpractice." Available from http://home.att.net/jbaugher4/f17.html. Internet. Accessed 27 February 2003.

Spinney, Franklin C. "Defense Time Bomb," March 6, 1996. Available from http://www.defense-and-society.org/fcs/pdf/defense_budget_time_bomb.pdf>. Internet. Accessed 6 February 2003.

Thompson, Loren B. "The Limits of Transformation." Washington Post, 12 March 2001.

Title 10 U.S.C. 2371. Section 845 of Public Law 103-160, FY1994 National Defense Authorization Act.

U.S. Department of the Army. 2002 U.S. Army Weapon Systems Handbook. Washington, D.C.: U.S. Department of the Army, 2002.

U.S. Department of the Army. The Army. Field Manual 1. Washington D.C.: U.S. Department of the Army, 14 June 2001.

U.S. General Accounting Office. <u>Best Practices: Capturing Design And Manufacturing Knowledge Early Improves Acquisition Outcomes</u>. GAO-02-701. Washington, D.C.: U.S. General Accounting Office, 15 July 2002.

U.S. General Accounting Office. <u>Defense Acquisition: DOD Faces Challenges in Implementing Best Practices</u>. GAO-02-469T. Washington, D.C.: U.S. General Accounting Office, 27 February 2002.

U.S. General Accounting Office. <u>Best Practices: Better Matching of Needs and Resources Will Lead to Better Weapon System Outcomes</u>. GAO-01-288. Washington, D.C. U.S. General Accounting Office, 8 March 2001.

U.S. General Accounting Office. <u>Best Practices: Better Management of Technology Development Can Improve Weapon System Outcomes</u>. GAO/NSIAD-99-162. Washington, D.C.: U.S. General Accounting Office, 30 July 1999.

U.S. General Accounting Office. <u>Defense Acquisition: Best Commercial Practices Can Improve Program Outcomes</u>. GAO/T-NSIAD-99-116. Washington, D.C.: U.S. General Accounting Office, 17 March 1999.

U.S. General Accounting Office. <u>Defense Acquisition: Improved Program Outcomes Are Possible</u>. GAO/T-NSIAD-98-123. Washington, D.C.: U.S. General Accounting Office, 18 March 1998.

U.S. General Accounting Office. <u>Defense Industry: Trends in DOD Spending, Industrial Productivity, and Competition</u>. GAO/T-PEMD-97-3. Washington, D.C.: U.S. General Accounting Office, 1997.

"US Army Selects GD To Lead Development of Land Warrior." Available from <http://www.defense-aerospace.com/data/communiques/data/2003Feb14176/>. Internet. Accessed 21 March 2003.

Velocci, Jr., Anthony L. "Pentagon Targeting Potential Suppliers." <u>Aviation Week & Space Technology</u>, 3 Februrary 2003.

Washington, William N. "A review of the Literature: Competitive Versus Sole-Source Procurements." <u>Acquisition Review Quarterly, Volume 4, Number 2</u> Alexandria, Defense Acquisition University, Spring 1997.

Weber, Rachel. <u>Swords Into Dow Shares, Governing the Decline of the Military Industrial Complex</u> Boulder: Westview Press, 2001.

Weston, Josh S. Co-Chairman, Business Executives for National Security Tail-to-Tooth Commission, Testimony to the Senate Budget Committee. Washington, D.C.: GPO, 2002.).

www.ingramcontent.com/pod-product-compliance
Lightning Source LLC
Chambersburg PA
CBHW081805280526
45789CB00008B/3003